D1321480

GREAT BRITISH ENGINEERING

CLAIRE THROP

raintree 🍃

a Capstone company — publishers for children

Raintree is an imprint of Capstone Global Library Limited, a company incorporated in England and Wales having its registered office at 264 Banbury Road, Oxford, OX2 7DY – Registered company number: 6695582

www.raintree.co.uk
myorders@raintree.co.uk

Edited by Helen Cox Cannons
Designed by Ted Williams and Kazuko Collins
Original illustrations © Capstone Global Library Limited 2018
Picture research by Svetlana Zhurkin
Production by Kathy McColley
Originated by Capstone Global Library Limited
Printed and bound in India

ISBN 978 1 4747 5912 0
22 21 20 19 18
10 9 8 7 6 5 4 3 2 1

British Library Cataloguing in Publication Data
A full catalogue record for this book is available from the British Library.

Acknowledgements
We would like to thank the following for permission to reproduce photographs:
Alamy: Paul Fearn, 20; Dreamstime: Karl Weller, cover (bottom left); Getty Images: David Madison, 27, Sygma/Bill Nation, 26; iStockphoto: duncan1890, 11, Gannet77, 15, ivan-96, 5, northlightimages, cover (top right), wcjohnston, 22; Newscom: Mirrorpix, 13, Zuma Press/Keystone Pictures USA, 16, 17; Shutterstock: Anna Kucherova, 21 (top), Claudio Divizia, 4, ColourArt, 21 (bottom), EOSMan, 19, Gary Perkin, 23 (top), Graham Bloomfield, 25, Harjit Samra, 6, IanC66, 24, Kamira, 9, Kiev.Victor, 8, MarcAndreLeTourneux, 7, Milind Arvind Ketka, cover (bottom right), Morphart Creation, 14, Paul Drabot, cover (top left), TreasureGalore, back cover, 7 (inset), Ulmus Media, 28, Vittorio Caramazza, 10; SuperStock: NaturePL, 12

Design Elements by Shutterstock

We would like to thank Martin Lewis for his invaluable help in the preparation of this book.

CONTENTS

Some words are shown in bold, **like this**. You can find out
what they mean by looking in the glossary.

INTRODUCTION

Britain takes up less than half a per cent of the world's land, but its engineers have achieved a huge number of successes. From canals to railways to ships to cars to planes, British engineers have created them all!

▼ The Clifton Suspension Bridge links Bristol and North Somerset.

FAST FACTS

Engineers

Civil engineers use maths and science to design and build roads, bridges and buildings. They solve problems, come up with ideas and then put them into practice. Mechanical engineers design and maintain machinery.

Industrial Revolution

During the mid-1700s and 1800s, British companies manufactured more and more, and the number of factories increased. This period in history became known as The Industrial Revolution.

Due to the increase in manufacturing, lots of changes came about. Towns got bigger and cities sprang up across the country. Because of this, a good transport system was needed to move goods around the country. In the mid- to late 1700s, canals were recognized as the best way to do this. "Canal mania" led to 39 new canals being ordered from 1792 to 1794. Then, in 1803–1804, Richard Trevithick invented the first locomotive at Pen-y-Darren iron mine, Merthyr Tydfil. Railways developed quickly after this, providing an even faster way of transporting goods.

All forms of transport, such as ships, canals and railways became stronger and faster. Designers and builders created more roads, bridges, tunnels and buildings. Britain became known as the "workshop of the world" because so many new inventions and engineering marvels were created.

▼ Richard Trevithick's locomotive was the first to do work. It carried several carriages full of iron and people in Wales in 1804.

▶ Pontcysyllte Aqueduct, 1795–1805

An aqueduct is an arched bridge that carries water above a gap or valley. Pontcysyllte Aqueduct in Wales is the longest and highest aqueduct in Britain. It has 19 arches and carries the Llangollen Canal above the River Dee. Thomas Telford designed the aqueduct nearly 40 metres above the river. The canal water runs through an iron **trough**, supported by stone **piers**.

▼ The aqueduct's piers are 38.7 metres high, but are hollow above 21.3 metres. This means that there is less pressure on the lower part of the pier.

BIOGRAPHY

Thomas Telford (1757–1834)

Thomas Telford was born in Dumfriesshire, Scotland. He became an engineer and moved to England. Telford created so many canals, buildings and bridges in Shropshire that a town was named after him: Telford. In 1820, he became president of the new Institution of Civil Engineers.

arms

troughs

axle

◀ The Falkirk Wheel is the only rotating boat lift in the world.

water-tight door

HOW IT WORKS

The Falkirk Wheel has two **steel** arms on each side of an axle (rod connecting two parts). Two steel water-filled troughs are supported between each pair of arms. The troughs each contain 250,000 litres of water, and they have watertight doors at each end. Each trough can take four 20-metre canal boats. They stay horizontal as the wheel turns.

▶ Falkirk Wheel, 2000–2002

The Falkirk Wheel was designed by British **architect** Tony Kettle and was built to connect two canals: the Forth and Clyde Canal and the Union Canal. The Union Canal is 25 metres higher than the Forth and Clyde Canal at Falkirk, the point where they meet. To get to the lift, boats travel along an aqueduct.

▶ London sewer system, 1859–1868

Drinking water for Londoners was taken from the River Thames. Until the mid-1800s, toilet waste was flushed straight into the Thames. Unsurprisingly, diseases, such as cholera, were common. Things came to a head in the summer of 1858. Very hot weather caused the smell of the dirty, **sewage**-filled River Thames to worsen. People called it the "Great Stink"!

Railway engineer Joseph Bazalgette was called in. He designed a new **sewer** system. This included 132 kilometres (82 miles) of tunnels running alongside the River Thames and 1,770 kilometres (1,100 miles) of street sewers. Bazalgette created the Victoria, Albert and Chelsea **embankments** to house the tunnels.

▼ Bazalgette designed the Abbey Mills sewage pumping station with Edmund Cooper and architect Charles Driver. It was built in 1868.

▶ Natural History Museum, 1873–1880

Alfred Waterhouse was responsible for designing the Natural History Museum in London. Sir Richard Owen, who founded the museum, wanted a "cathedral to nature". So Waterhouse included carvings of animals in the building's design. The building itself looks just like a **Gothic** cathedral.

▶ "Gherkin", 2001–2003

British **architect** Sir Norman Foster's company designed 30 St Mary Axe, also known as the "Gherkin". It is an environmentally friendly office building. It uses half the energy that a rectangular tall building would use.

▶ Thirty-five kilometres in length of **steel** was used to build the Gherkin.

HOW IT WORKS

The outside of the building is all glass. Six triangular lightwells allow natural light to enter far into the building. These design features keep lighting costs down. There are open panels in the lightwells that allow air in from outside. This reduces the need for air-conditioning, which uses up a lot of energy.

▶ SS *Great Britain*, 1839–1843

Isambard Kingdom Brunel's SS *Great Britain* was the first ship to be built from **wrought iron**. Many people did not think that a ship made of metal would be able to float. However, in 1845 the ship made its first trip to the United States – without sinking.

Brunel included a screw **propeller** rather than paddles to increase the ship's speed. The engine was 1,000 **horsepower**. This new shipping technology meant that the *Great Britain* was the fastest ship on the sea.

▲ The SS *Great Britain* was also the longest ship, at 100 metres long.

Isambard Kingdom Brunel
(1806–1859)

From a young age, Isambard Kingdom Brunel worked on some great engineering projects. He was only 24 when his design was chosen for a bridge to cross the River Avon in Bristol: the Clifton Suspension Bridge. He was also responsible for the Great Western Railway, which connects London and Bristol.

▲ Isambard Kingdom Brunel

▶ SS *Great Eastern*, 1854–1858

The groundbreaking SS *Great Eastern* was Brunel's third ship. It was the largest ship ever built, at 211 metres long. It was built to take people to India and Australia without having to stop to refuel.

▶ RRS *Discovery*, 1900

The Dundee Shipbuilders Company built *Discovery* for the British National Antarctic Expedition. It was the first scientific research ship. *Discovery* was based on whalers, which are ships used to hunt whales in the Arctic. The engineers made a number of changes in the design, however.

▶ RRS *Discovery*

HOW IT WAS BUILT

Discovery was made of wood. This was because magnetic surveys were to be carried out. No iron or **steel** could be within 9 metres of the area. Otherwise the metal could affect the readings. No portholes were added to the sides of the ship. The pressure of the ice would have turned the portholes into areas of weakness, possibly causing the ship's hull to break apart. The rudder and propeller used to steer and drive the ship could be lifted into the hull. This was so that the ice would not damage them.

▶ HMS *Dreadnought,* 1905–1906

HMS *Dreadnought* was revolutionary. It was the best-armed and fastest battleship ever built. It had 10 12-inch (305-millimetre) guns, 24 3-inch (76-millimetre) guns, 5 machine guns and 4 torpedo tubes (for launching torpedoes). In contrast, HMS *King Edward VII*, a ship completed just one year before, had only 4 big guns, 10 smaller guns and 4 torpedoes.

Dreadnought was also faster than other battleships, reaching a top speed of 21 **knots**. *King Edward VII* could only reach 18.5 knots. This extra speed was achieved by using **steam turbines** instead of **piston** engines. At larger sizes, turbines were more efficient at converting steam to energy.

▼ In 1915, during World War I, *Dreadnought* became the only battleship to sink a submarine.

TRAINS AND RAILWAYS

▶ Liverpool to Manchester Railway, 1826–1830

George Stephenson was the engineer for the Liverpool to Manchester Railway. At the time, trains were slow, not very reliable and used too much coal. The railway's owners set up a competition to create a better train. Stephenson and his son, Robert, came up with *Rocket*. The train won the competition!

FAST FACTS

Why did *Rocket* win?

Instead of using just one large tube to heat the water that would provide the steam to move the train, *Rocket* used 25 smaller tubes. This meant the water boiled faster because there was a larger heated surface in contact with the water. Exhaust steam was also rerouted from the cylinder to the chimney. This meant the fire could burn more strongly, creating more steam and therefore more power.

▼ Stephenson's *Rocket*

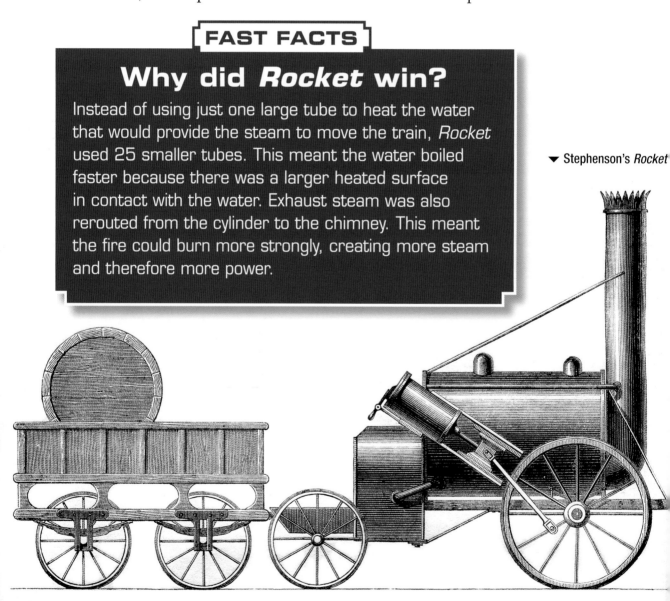

George Stephenson (1781–1848)

George Stephenson worked in coalmines when he was young. He was often in charge of the steam engines in the mines. He created his first locomotive for carrying coal in 1814. In 1821, he was chosen to create the first public railway: the Stockton and Darlington Railway. Stephenson is known as the "father of railways".

▲ The *Flying Scotsman* stopped running in 1963, but it has recently been restored and is back on the tracks.

▶ *Flying Scotsman*, 1922–1923

The *Flying Scotsman* made the first non-stop train journey from London to Edinburgh in 1928. At the time, it was the longest express route in the world. Designed by Sir Nigel Gresley, the *Flying Scotsman* was the first train to reach 160 kilometres (100 miles) per hour, in 1934. It had a much larger boiler than older trains.

▶ London Underground, 1860–1863

The London Underground was the world's first underground railway. A growing number of people were travelling by horse and carriage for business in the City of London. The City of London was the financial centre of London. This made the city streets very busy. **Solicitor** Charles Pearson came up with the idea for an underground railway to reduce road traffic. The underground linked the major railway stations of Paddington, Euston and Kings Cross with the City. The first section was the Metropolitan line between Paddington and Farringdon.

HOW IT WAS BUILT

John Fowler (who later worked on the Forth Bridge – see page 20) was the engineer in charge of the project. The Underground was not built using a lot of machinery. Rather, men known as "navvies" worked with picks and shovels. For the first section, they used the cut and cover method to make the train tunnels. The navvies dug up an existing road to create a trench and laid railway tracks. They then built brick walls along the sides and added a roof over the trench. Finally, they put the roads back over the top.

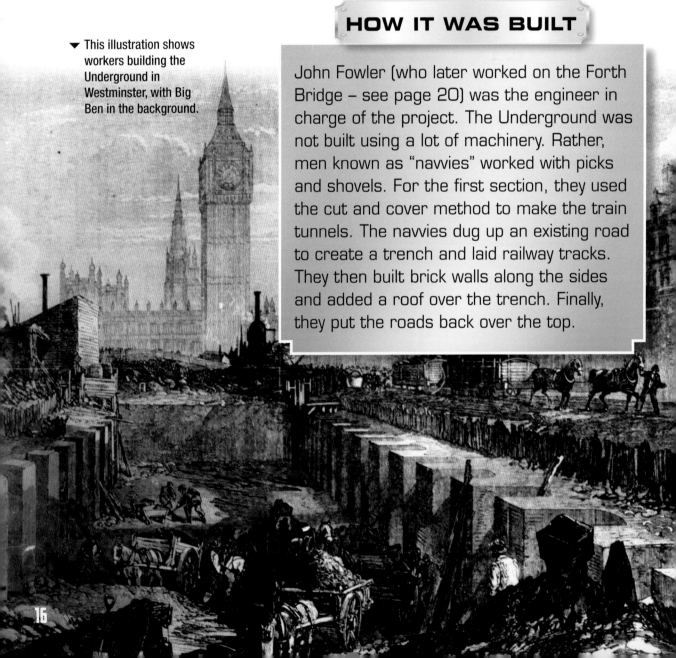

▼ This illustration shows workers building the Underground in Westminster, with Big Ben in the background.

▲ More than nine million people travelled on the Underground in its first year.

The Underground changes London

The Underground made a huge impact on London. It meant that all the collection of villages that surrounded the City of London gradually joined to become one large city. *The Times* newspaper said the Underground was "the great engineering triumph of the day". Underground trains were steam-driven engines to start with. In 1890, the City and South London line became the first underground railway to have electric trains.

BRIDGES

▶ Menai Suspension Bridge, 1818–1826

At the time it was built, the Menai Suspension Bridge was the longest bridge **span** in the world. In 1800, Ireland joined Great Britain in the Act of Union. The new bridge was needed to cope with the increase in people travelling between London and Ireland. This was because Holyhead was the port where people caught boats to and from Ireland. The only way to get over the **strait** was by ferry. The new bridge reduced people's travel time greatly.

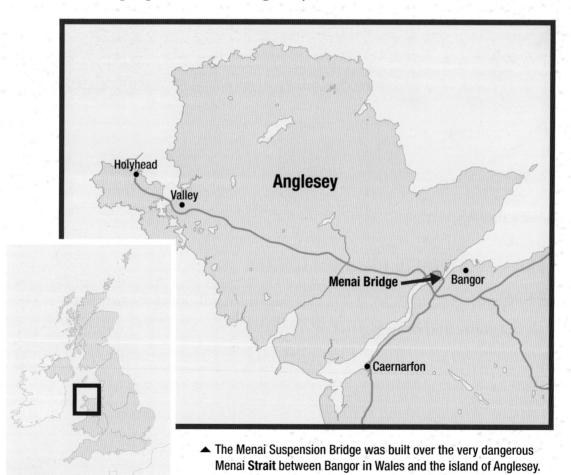

▲ The Menai Suspension Bridge was built over the very dangerous Menai **Strait** between Bangor in Wales and the island of Anglesey.

chains

rods

towers

▲ The Menai Suspension Bridge

The bridge had to be built high enough to allow tall ships to sail underneath. Engineer Thomas Telford suggested a suspension bridge. Suspension bridges were not new, but none had been built on this scale before. Two towers supported the central bridge span. The towers were linked to stone arches and **piers** at each side.

HOW IT WAS BUILT

First the arches, piers and towers were built from limestone. Tunnels were driven into the rock on each side of the strait. Huge 3-metre-long bolts held down the ends of 16 giant chains. The chains were hung in loops from each tower across the water. They held up the bridge's 176-metre-long central span. The wooden road surface was laid on iron bars. These were connected to the 16 chains by **wrought iron** rods.

▶ Forth Bridge, 1882–1889

The Forth Bridge in Scotland was the longest cantilever bridge in the world at the time it was built. It runs across the Firth of Forth, between Lothian and Fife. It was the first major structure in Britain to be made of **steel**. Sir John Fowler and Sir Benjamin Baker came up with the cantilever design.

▲ Sir John Fowler and Sir Benjamin Baker demonstrated how a cantilever bridge works in 1887. Kaichi Watanabe, an engineer who also worked on the Bridge, is in the centre.

Caissons

Caissons are watertight chambers that allow people to work under water. These had to be put in place first. Then workers built granite piers on top to support the bridge's three double cantilevers. Each one is 110 metres high. The cantilevers were joined together by long steel **girders**.

HOW IT WORKS

A cantilever is a long piece of metal or wood that sticks out sideways from a support. To hold the cantilever of a bridge in place, engineers have to use a very heavy weight called a counterweight. Think of a ruler on the edge of a table. If it goes too far over the edge, it falls off. By placing something heavy (a counterweight) on one end, the ruler can stick out much further over the edge of the table than it would do otherwise.

▲ The Forth Bridge

cantilevers

▶ Gateshead Millennium Bridge, 1998–2001

The Gateshead Millennium Bridge is the world's first tilting bridge. **Architect** Keith Brownlie designed it. The River Tyne is a busy shipping route, so the bridge moves vertically to allow room for ships to go underneath it. It is powered by eight electric motors.

▼ The Gateshead Millennium Bridge cost a total of £22 million to build.

Millennium Bridge

▶ Box Tunnel, 1836–1841

Box Tunnel was part of Isambard Kingdom Brunel's Great Western Railway, running between Chippenham and Bath. At the time it was built, it was the longest railway tunnel at 2.9 kilometres (1.8 miles) long. Using only candles to see, 1500 men worked 24 hours a day on the tunnel. This rose to 4,000 men towards the finishing stages.

▼ Box Tunnel

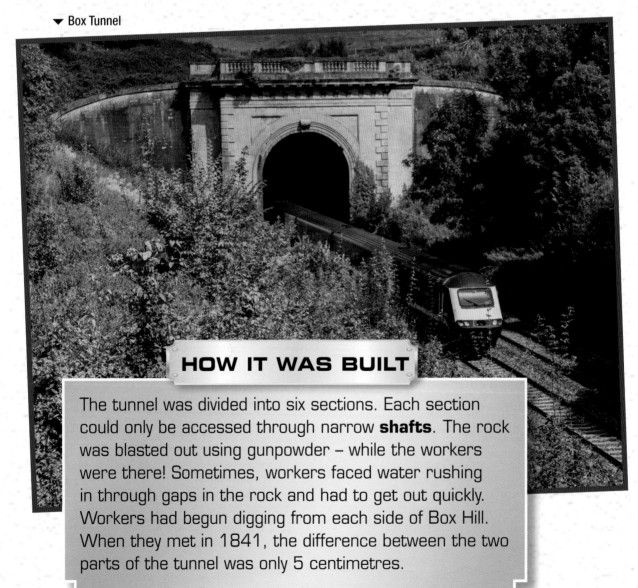

HOW IT WAS BUILT

The tunnel was divided into six sections. Each section could only be accessed through narrow **shafts**. The rock was blasted out using gunpowder – while the workers were there! Sometimes, workers faced water rushing in through gaps in the rock and had to get out quickly. Workers had begun digging from each side of Box Hill. When they met in 1841, the difference between the two parts of the tunnel was only 5 centimetres.

◀ Tunnel-boring machine

▶ Channel Tunnel, 1987–1994

The Channel Tunnel was a joint British–French project. It is the longest undersea rail tunnel in the world at 37.9 kilometres (23.5 miles). Diggers worked from Britain and France at the same time. When they met up, there was only 1.9 centimetres difference in the tunnels' positions.

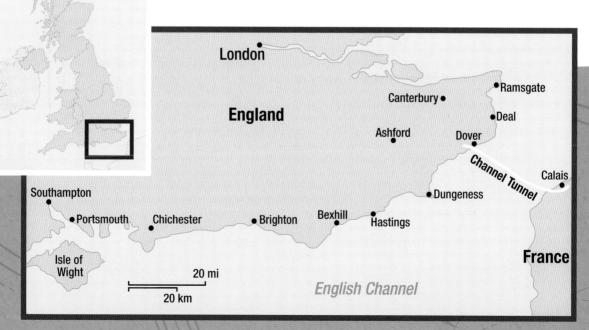

London

England

Canterbury

Ramsgate

Deal

Ashford

Dover

Channel Tunnel

Calais

Southampton

Portsmouth Chichester Brighton Bexhill Hastings Dungeness

Isle of Wight

20 mi

20 km

English Channel

France

▲ One of the Spitfire's great strengths in battle was that it could perform well when high in the sky. Later models could fly as high as 12,2000 metres (40,000 feet).

▶ Spitfire, 1934–1936

The Spitfire was a single-seat fighter aircraft used by the Royal Air Force (RAF) with great success in World War II (1939–1945). R.J. Mitchell was the designer. The original design made it easy to upgrade the aircraft with new engines and guns. After Mitchell's death in 1937, designer Joe Smith made the Spitfire even more powerful.

HOW IT WAS BUILT

The plane was very strong and adaptable. There was even a bulge in the **cockpit** for taller pilots! A Spitfire's wings were elliptical, or oval. This helped it to climb higher and turn faster in the sky than other planes. Battle of Britain (1940) Spitfires could reach a speed of 580 kilometres (360 miles) per hour. Later models were able to fly at 710 kilometres (440 miles) per hour. The original Spitfire had eight machine guns. These could fire 160 rounds every second. Later versions of the Spitfire had larger engines, so were even faster. They also carried cannons as well as machine guns.

BIOGRAPHY

R.J. MITCHELL (1895–1937)

British aircraft designer R.J. Mitchell worked at Supermarine Aviation Works in Southampton from 1916 until his death. His main job for the company was to design seaplanes, which were used for racing. One of these planes broke the world speed record in 1929. Mitchell based the Spitfire on this seaplane.

▶ Concorde, 1962–1976

Concorde was the first – and only – supersonic passenger jet. It achieved world record flight times between Europe and the United States. It was a joint project between Britain and France. Sir James Hamilton was the plane's designer. By 2003, environmental worries – about the amount of fuel each flight used and how noisy it was – meant that Concorde was no longer used.

◀ The triangle shape of Concorde's wings is different from other planes. The shape reduces **air resistance**, which allows the plane to move at a faster speed.

▲ The "SSC" in the name ThrustSSC stands for SuperSonic Car.

▶ ThrustSSC, 1994–1997

Richard Noble's ThrustSSC was the first land vehicle to break the **sound barrier**, or travel faster than sound. When cars get close to the speed of sound, they can start to take off, a bit like a plane. This would result in a crash – something to be avoided at over 1,126 kilometres (700 miles) per hour!

HOW IT WAS BUILT

The shape of the car was important. It had to be **streamlined** to reduce air resistance. This meant the steering of the car had to come from the back wheels rather than the front ones. The back wheels were placed one in front of the other to keep the streamlined shape. The car had two engines, providing 110,000 **horsepower**. This gave it the same amount of power as 145 Formula One racing cars.

Computers and models

Ron Ayers, a member of the ThrustSSC team, is an aerodynamicist. He studies the movement of vehicles or other solid objects through air. To work out how to build a car that could travel faster than sound, he had to use a computer to reproduce the conditions in which the car would be driven. Then engineers made and tested a rocket-powered model of the car. Luckily, the results matched up and the car was built.

▼ Jet fighter pilot Andy Green drove fast enough to break the sound barrier in October 1997 at Black Rock Desert in the United States. ThrustSSC reached a speed of just over 1,228 kilometres (763 miles) per hour.

CONCLUSION

British engineers have made stunning engineering projects for hundreds of years. This success continues today. Queensferry Crossing (2011–2016) is the third bridge to cross the Forth of Firth in Scotland. It measures 2.7 kilometres (1.7 miles), and is the longest three-tower, **cable-stayed bridge** in the world. It was built as the main roadway for vehicles travelling between Edinburgh and the county of Fife.

▼ The Queensferry Crossing opened in August 2017.

In 2017, engineers completed new flood defences in Leeds. These involve moveable **weirs** that can be lowered after heavy rain. They reduce river levels and prevent flooding. It is the first time that moveable weirs have been used in Britain.

These and many other engineering projects mean that Britain continues to move forward into the future. British engineers continue to push the limits to produce the next great engineering success.

TIMELINE

1790

1803–1804 First train at Pen-y-Darren mine, Merthyr Tydfil — **1800**

1795–1805 Pontcysyllte Aqueduct

1810

1820

1818–1826 Menai Suspension Bridge

1826–1830 Liverpool to Manchester Railway and the *Rocket*

1830

1836–1841 Box Tunnel

1839–1843 SS *Great Britain*

1840

1850

1854–1858 SS *Great Eastern*

1860

1860–1863 London Underground (Metropolitan Railway)

1859–1868 London sewers

1870

1873–1880 Natural History Museum

1880

1882–1889 Forth Bridge

1890

1900 RRS *Discovery* — **1900**

1905–1906 HMS *Dreadnought*

1910

1920

1922–1923 *Flying Scotsman*

1930

1934–1936 Spitfire

1940

1950

1960

1962–1976 Concorde

1970

1980

1987–1994 Channel Tunnel

1990

1998–2001 Gateshead Millennium Bridge

1994–1997 ThrustSSC

2000

2001–2003 30 St Mary Axe (the "Gherkin")

2000–2002 Falkirk Wheel

2010

2011–2016 Queensferry Crossing

2015–2017 Moveable weir flood defences, Leeds

2020

GLOSSARY

air resistance force of air rubbing against things, which slows down moving vehicles

architect person who designs buildings

cable-stayed bridge type of suspension bridge, in which the supporting cables are attached to the roadway

cockpit place in an aeroplane or car in which the pilot or driver sits

embankment thick wall of earth or other material, such as stone or concrete. It is built to carry a road, railway line or sewer over an area of low ground.

girder long, thick piece of steel that is used in the building of bridges

Gothic style of building based on those created in medieval times (1100s to 1500s). They included tall columns, high curved ceilings and pointed arches.

horsepower measure of power, used to measure the power of an engine

hull frame or body of a ship or aircraft

knot measure of speed used by ships and aircraft. One knot is about the same as 1.85 kilometres (1.15 miles) per hour.

pier pillar that holds heavy loads

piston small tube that moves up and down inside a larger tube to generate power

propeller device with spinning blades

sewage waste matter

sewers series of tunnels that carry away waste, usually underground

shaft vertical (up and down) passageway

solicitor person whose job it is to give legal advice to clients, prepare legal cases and represent clients in court

sound barrier breaking the sound barrier means travelling faster than the speed of sound

span part of something, such as a bridge or arch, between two supports

steam turbine piece of machinery that uses steam to spin blades in order to create energy, for example to power a propeller

steel strong metal, made mostly from iron and a small amount of carbon and another substance

strait narrow strip of sea

streamlined designed to move easily and quickly through air

trough narrow channel

weir low barrier built across a river that is used to control the flow of water

wrought iron type of iron that is easy to bend and shape

FIND OUT MORE

Books

A History of Britain in 12 Feats of Engineering, Paul Rockett (Franklin Watts, 2015)

Bridges (Awesome Engineering), Sally Spray (Franklin Watts, 2017)

The Railway Revolution, Jo Nelson (Collins, 2016)

Websites

www.bbc.co.uk/education/clips/z4fvr82
This BBC education video gives a quick visual guide to the developments in transport during the Victorian era.

www.dkfindout.com/uk/transport/history-aircraft/concorde
Find out more about Concorde on this web page.

PLACES TO VISIT

As well as visiting some of the ships, canals, bridges and buildings mentioned in this book, you could also go to the museums that house some of the transport mentioned.

Coventry Transport Museum
Millennium Place
Hales Street
Coventry CV1 1JD
www.transport-museum.com
Visit this museum to see ThrustSSC, as well as many other vehicles.

National Railway Museumn
Leeman Road
York YO26 4XJ
www.nrm.org.uk
This museum has a working copy of Stephenson's *Rocket*.

INDEX